Perennial Pleasures

Reflections on Flowers & Gardens

THE METROPOLITAN MUSEUM OF ART
NEW YORK

All of the works of art reproduced in this book are from the collections of The Metropolitan Museum of Art.

FRONT COVER BORDER: Adaptation of a design for an embroidered photograph frame
Morris & Co., British, ca. 1900
Watercolor on paper
Gift of Harry G. Friedman, 1964   64.682.345

FRONT COVER: Detail of a Sèvres porcelain plaque for a secretary
French, soft-paste porcelain, ca. 1790
Gift of Samuel H. Kress Foundation, 1958 58.75.57

BACK COVER: Detail of a Sèvres porcelain plant pot
French, soft-paste porcelain, 1759
Gift of Barbara Lowe Fallass, 1964 64.159.2a

TITLE PAGE: *Pansies on a Table*
Henri Matisse, French, 1869–1954
Oil on paper, mounted on wood, ca. 1918–19
Bequest of Joan Whitney Payson, 1975   1976.201.22

PAGE 5: *Peonies*
Édouard Manet, French, 1832–1883
Oil on canvas, 1864
Bequest of Joan Whitney Payson, 1975 1976.201.16

Published by The Metropolitan Museum of Art

Copyright © 1993 by The Metropolitan Museum of Art

First Edition
Printed in Hong Kong
09 08 07 06 05 04 03 02 01 00   7 6 5 4 3

Produced by the Department of Special Publications, The Metropolitan Museum of Art
Designed by Miriam Berman
Cover designed by Anna Raff

Visit the Museum's Web site: www.metmuseum.org

ISBN 0-87099-659-2

Library of Congress Catalog Card Number: 93-077018

INTRODUCTION

"If I had but two loaves of bread, I would sell one and buy hyacinths, for they would feed my soul," said the thirteenth-century Persian poet Saʿdi. Seven hundred years later, the American wit Dorothy Parker concurred: "They that have roses never need bread." And haven't we all splurged on an irresistible bouquet when we perhaps should have saved our pennies? As the quotations and pictures in this book reveal, the appeal of flowers is virtually universal, and the pleasures they afford are perennial.

From medieval textiles to Islamic manuscripts, from Japanese prints to Impressionist paintings, from sermons to sonnets, and from nonsense verse to haiku, arts and letters through the ages have been inspired by flowers. Some painters, like Henri Fantin-Latour, seem challenged to reproduce flowers' colors, translucence, and delicate forms. Others are drawn to explore their allure: In her intense portraits of blossoms, Georgia O'Keeffe seems to be penetrating the very mysteries of nature. Among writers, A. A. Milne reveals a friendliness and familiarity with the cheering presence of flowers, while Wordsworth seems nearly overwhelmed by their beauty or their inherent profundity. "I feel really frightened when I sit down to paint a flower," said the Pre-Raphaelite painter Holman Hunt, yet his nerves didn't stop him, or other artists over the years.

To grow flowers, to create a garden from dirt and seed, is deeply satisfying. The American essayist Charles Dudley Warner claimed that "the man who has planted a garden feels he has done something for the good of the whole world." Some of the writers and painters represented in this book were themselves avid gardeners. Claude Monet created his gardens at Giverny with the same eye for beauty with which he made his paintings. George C. Lambdin grew flowers and then painted them. Vita Sackville-West was perhaps more famous for her gardens at Sissinghurst Castle and her articles about them than for her novels and poems. Other horticultural writers, like Celia Thaxter, wrote so beautifully about their gardens that their works have been acknowledged as fine literature. And in China and Japan, gardens rank as high art and are fitting subjects for pictures and poems.

But gardening is arduous, sometimes onerous, work. Warner also admitted that it required "a cast-iron back with a hinge on it." And not everyone has a knack for it—like Ogden Nash, you may be "a horticultural ignoramus." Green thumb or black, aesthete or boor, however, everyone can admire and appreciate flowers and gardens. The words and images that follow capture the essence of flowers and our affection for them. Whether you have a thriving, burgeoning garden or a few pots on a windowsill, whether you make elegant, elaborate arrangements or buy a bunch of daisies on the way home from work, here is a book to feed your soul.

CAROLYN VAUGHAN

四十雀

四十から君まえてていまきみかもちすてつまみ
これとり

これとり

安静敦丸

林泰之道

これらくりの名のところちはさひり形 色えれまほとやせもき刀

The flowers appear on the earth; the time of the singing of birds is come . . .

SONG OF SOLOMON 2:12

*Japanese Robin and Chickadee
with Chrysanthemums*
Kitagawa Utamaro
Japanese, 1753–1806
Polychrome woodblock print
from *Momochidori (Various Birds),*
ca. 1790
Rogers Fund, 1918
Japanese book no. 43

The first flower that blossomed on this earth
was an invitation to the unborn song.

RABINDRANATH TAGORE
(1861–1941)

Hummingbird and Passionflowers
Martin Johnson Heade
American, 1819–1904
Oil on canvas
Gift of Alfred Weatherby, 1946
46.17

Nothing is more the child of art than a garden.

SIR WALTER SCOTT
(1771–1832)

Bridge over a Pool of Water Lilies
Claude Monet
French, 1840–1926
Oil on canvas, 1899
H. O. Havemeyer Collection
Bequest of Mrs. H. O.
Havemeyer, 1929
29.100.113

10

... what greater delight is there than to behold the earth apparelled with plants, as with a robe of embroidered work, set with Orient pearls and garnished with great diversity of rare and costly jewels?

JOHN GERARD
(1545–1612)

Musical Garden Party
English, third quarter of the
17th century
Silk embroidery on canvas
Gift of Irwin Untermyer, 1964
64.101.1314

He who is born with a silver spoon in his mouth is generally considered a fortunate person, but his good fortune is small compared to that of the happy mortal who enters this world with a passion for flowers in his soul.

CELIA THAXTER
(1835–1894)

Lilacs and Peonies
Suzanne Valadon
French, 1867–1938
Oil on canvas, 1929
Bequest of Miss Adelaide Milton
de Groot (1876–1967), 1967
67.187.112

If you want to be happy for a week, take a wife.
If you want to be happy all your life, make a garden.

CHINESE PROVERB

Planting Chrysanthemums
Lu Chih
Chinese, 1496–1576
(Ming dynasty)
Detail from a hanging scroll, ink
and pale color on paper
Edward Elliott Family Collection,
Gift of Douglas Dillon, 1986
1986.266.3

My garden will never
   make me famous
I'm a horticultural
   ignoramus,
I can't tell a string bean
   from a soy bean
Or even a girl bean
   from a boy bean.

OGDEN NASH
(1902–1971)

King's Cookham Rise
Stanley Spencer
British, 1891–1959
Oil on canvas, 1947
Purchase, Lila Acheson Wallace
Gift, 1981
1981.193

19

The flower in the vase still smiles, but no longer laughs.

MALCOLM DE CHAZAL
(b. 1902)

Mount Fuji and Flowers
David Hockney
British, b. 1937
Acrylic on canvas, 1972
Purchase, Mrs. Arthur Hays
Sulzberger Gift, 1972
1972.128

Fig. 156.   Fig. 160.

Published as the Act directs, Aug.ᵗ 1, 1798, by N. Heideloff, at the Gallery of Fashion, N.º 90, Wardour Street.

A flower unplucked is but left to the falling,
And nothing is gained by not gathering roses.

ROBERT FROST
(1874–1963)

Large Sunflowers I
Emil Nolde
German, 1867–1956
Oil on wood, 1928
Bequest of Walter J. Reinemann, 1970
1970.213

Flowers have an expression
of countenance as much as
men or animals. Some seem
to smile; some have a sad
expression; some are pensive
and diffident; others again
are plain, honest, and upright,
like the broad-faced sunflower
and the hollyhock.

HENRY WARD BEECHER
(1813–1887)

The Persian king is zealously cared for, so that he may find gardens wherever he goes. Their name is Paradise, and they are full of all things fair and good that the earth can bring forth.

XENOPHON
(ca. 431–ca. 352 B.C.)

Garden of Perfume
Leaf from a Būstān of Sa'di
Persian, Bokhara School,
16th century
Ink, colors, and gold on paper
Frederick C. Hewitt Fund, 1911
11.134.2

They spoke no word,
The visitor, the host,
And the white chrysanthemum.

JAPANESE

The Shadows on the Wall "Chrysanthemums"
Baron Adolph de Meyer
American (b. France),
1868–1946
Gelatin silver print, ca. 1906
Alfred Stieglitz Collection, 1933
33.43.231

I know nothing so pleasant as to sit there on a summer afternoon, with the western sun flickering through the great elder-tree, and lighting up our gay parterres, where flowers and flowering shrubs are set as thick as grass in a field, a wilderness of blossom, interwoven, intertwined, wreathy, garlandy, profuse beyond all profusion . . .

MARY MITFORD
(1787–1855)

Garden of the Painter at St. Clair
Henri-Edmond Cross
French, 1856–1910
Watercolor
Robert Lehman Collection, 1975
1975.1.590

Now every field is clothed with grass, and every tree with leaves; now the woods put forth their blossoms, and the year assumes its gay attire.

VIRGIL
(70–19 B.C.)

The Flowering Orchard
Vincent van Gogh
Dutch, 1853–1890
Oil on canvas, 1888
The Mr. and Mrs. Henry Ittleson,
Jr. Purchase Fund, 1956
56.13

To dig and delve in nice clean dirt
Can do a mortal little hurt.

JOHN KENDRICK BANGS
(1862–1922)

Allegory of Earth: Two Children Gardening
François Boucher
French, 1703–1770
Black chalk, heightened with
white chalk, on brown paper
Louis V. Bell Fund, 1964
64.281.1

W̲on't you come
into my garden?
I would like my
roses to see you.

RICHARD SHERIDAN
(1751–1816)

Garden at Sainte-Adresse
Claude Monet
French, 1840–1926
Oil on canvas
Purchased with special
contributions and purchase
funds given or bequeathed by
friends of the Museum, 1967
67.241

A morning-glory at my window satisfies me more than the metaphysics of books.

WALT WHITMAN
(1819–1892)

A Nocturne
John La Farge
American, 1835–1910
Watercolor, gouache, and
charcoal on off-white wove
paper, ca. 1885
Bequest of Louise Veltin, 1937
37.104

Figures in a Persian Garden
Persian (Isfahan), first quarter of
the 17th century
Tile wall panel; composite body,
glaze-painted
Rogers Fund, 1903
03.9b

In eastern lands they talk in flowers,
and tell in a garland their loves and cares.

JAMES GATES PERCIVAL
(1795–1856)

There is a garden in every childhood, an enchanted place where colors are brighter, the air softer, and the morning more fragrant than ever again.

ELIZABETH LAWRENCE
(1910–1985)

Cottage Garden, Warwick, England
Edmund H. Garrett
American, 1853–1929
Watercolor, gouache, and
graphite on off-white wove paper
Gift of Mr. and Mrs. Stuart P.
Feld, 1977
1977.426

What a delight it is
When, of a morning,
I get up and go out
To find in full bloom a flower
That yesterday was not there.

TACHIBANA AKEMI
(1812–1868)

The Garden at Vaucresson
Édouard Vuillard
French, 1868–1940
Distemper on canvas, 1923 and 1927
Catharine Lorillard Wolfe
Collection, Wolfe Fund, 1952
52.183

The beauteous pansies rise
In purple, gold, and blue,
With tints of rainbow hue
Mocking the sunset skies.

THOMAS J. OUSELEY
(d. 1874)

Still Life with Pansies
Henri Fantin-Latour
French, 1836–1904
Oil on canvas, 1874
The Mr. and Mrs. Henry Ittleson,
Jr. Purchase Fund, 1966
66.194

People from a planet without flowers would think
we must be mad with joy the whole time to have
such things about us.

IRIS MURDOCH
(b. 1919)

Nasturtiums with "Dance"
Henri Matisse
French, 1869–1954
Oil on canvas, 1912
Bequest of Scofield Thayer, 1982
1984.433.16

Though a life of retreat offers various joys,
None, I think will compare with the time one employs
In the study of herbs, or in striving to gain
Some practical knowledge of nature's domain.
Get a garden! What kind you may get matters not.

ABBOT WALAFRID STRABO
809(?)–849

H ow often I regret that plants cannot talk.

Fleur de Lis
Robert Lewis Reid
American, 1862–1929
Oil on canvas, ca. 1895–1900
George A. Hearn Fund, 1907
07.140

Cherry Blossom Viewing
Kitagawa Utamaro, Japanese, 1753–1806
Polychrome woodblock print from *Fugen-Azo: The Goddess of Integrity,* 1790
Rogers Fund, 1918   Japanese book no. 49

Three brief days and lo! the whole world is full of cherry blossoms.

JAPANESE PROVERB

There is probably no inanimate object in the world more beautiful than a delicately tinted Rose. There is certainly nothing else which combines such beauty of form and color with such exquisite delicacy of texture and such delicious perfume . . . . The charm seems to me to lie, in great part, in the fine silky texture of the petals and in their translucency. . . . It is the charm which it shares with every beautiful thing which is "hidden yet half revealed."

GEORGE C. LAMBDIN
(1830–1896)

Roses
George C. Lambdin
American, 1830–1896
Oil on wood, 1878
Gift of Mrs. Manfred P. Welcher, 1918
18.116

We cannot fathom the mystery of a single flower,
nor is it intended that we should . . .

JOHN RUSKIN
(1819–1900)

Black Hollyhock, Blue Larkspur
Georgia O'Keeffe
American, 1887–1986
Oil on canvas, 1929
George A. Hearn Fund, 1934
34.51

Spring (Fruit Trees in Bloom)
Claude Monet, French, 1840–1926
Oil on canvas, 1873
Bequest of Mary Livingston Willard, 1926   26.186.1

Even if I knew certainly the world would end tomorrow,
I would plant an apple tree today.

MARTIN LUTHER
(1483–1546)

To me the meanest flower that blows can give
Thoughts that do often lie too deep for tears.

WILLIAM WORDSWORTH
(1770–1850)

Thistle
John Singer Sargent
American, 1856–1925
Watercolor on paper
Gift of Mrs. Francis Ormond, 1950
50.130.141aa

. . . a lovely clump of dwarf iris, whose name I believe
to be Iris *histrio*, though I am not quite sure, deep blue,
freckled with brilliant gold spots, are sunning themselves
with the utmost self-complacency.

ALFRED AUSTIN
(1835–1913)

Crested Dwarf Iris, Great Smoky
Mountains National Park, Tennessee, 1968
Eliot Porter
American, 1901–1990
Dye-transfer print
Gift of Eliot Porter, 1975
1985.1033.1

Chantons sur lelette
auec ta musette
quelque note doulce

For now the fragrant
flowers do spring and
sprout in seemly sort,
The little birds
do sit and sing,
the lambs do
make fine sport …
The lords and ladies
now abroad,
for their disport
and play,
Do kiss sometimes
upon the grass,
and sometimes
in the hay.

FRANCIS BEAUMONT (1584–1616)
AND JOHN FLETCHER (1579–1625)

*"Millefleurs" Tapestry with Shepherd
and Shepherdess Making Music*
Southern Netherlands, 1500–30
Wool and silk
Bequest of Susan Vanderpoel
Clark, 1967
67.155.8

I have banished all worldly care from my garden;
it is a clean and open spot.

HSIEH LING-YÜN
(385–433)

Cottage Beside the Wu-t'ung Tree
Attributed to Wen Po-jen
Chinese, 1502–1575
(Ming dynasty)
Detail from a hanging scroll,
ink and light color on paper
Gift of Mr. and Mrs. Earl Morse, 1972
1972.278.3

A house with daffodils in it is a house lit up,
whether or no the sun be shining outside.
Daffodils in a green bowl—and let it snow if it will.

A. A. MILNE
(1882–1956)

Small Daffodils
Charles Demuth
American, 1883–1935
Watercolor on paper
Alfred Stieglitz Collection, 1949
49.70.63

Long-stemmed roses,
their buds closed like eggs,
then open all of a sudden,
roses in the heart of Paris
awakened by the rainbow
trapped in a spray of water...

COLETTE
(1873–1954)

Still Life with Roses and Fruit
Henri Fantin-Latour
French, 1836–1904
Oil on canvas, 1863
Bequest of Alice A. Hay, 1987
1987.119

I cannot see
which is which:
the glowing
plum blossom *is*
the spring night's moon.

IZUMI SHIKIBU
(974–1034)

Girl with Lantern on a Balcony at Night
Suzuki Haronobu
Japanese, 1725–1770
Polychrome woodblock print, ca. 1768
Fletcher Fund, 1929
JP 1506

Ever since I could remember anything, flowers have been like dear friends to me, comforters, inspirers, powers to uplift and to cheer.

CELIA THAXTER
(1835–1894)

Mauve Primulas on a Table
Sir William Nicholson
British, 1872–1949
Oil on wood, 1927
Bequest of Mary Cushing
Fosburgh, 1978
1979.135.15

JULIAN CLARENCE LEVI.

A garden is not for giving or taking. A garden is for all.

FRANCES HODGSON BURNETT
(1849–1924)

Garden, Camp Highwall,
Lake Placid, New York
Julian Levi
American, 1874–1971
Watercolor over pencil on
off-white wove paper, 1942
Bequest of Julian Clarence Levi, 1971
1971.200.6